All Kinds of

Bodies

Written by Judith Heneghan

Illustrated by Ayesha Rubio
and Jenny Palmer

CRABTREE
PUBLISHING COMPANY
WWW.CRABTREEBOOKS.COM

CRABTREE
PUBLISHING COMPANY
WWW.CRABTREEBOOKS.COM

Author: Judith Heneghan

Editorial director: Kathy Middleton

Editors: Nicola Edwards, Ellen Rodger

Illustrators: Ayesha Rubio, Jenny Palmer

Proofreader: Crystal Sikkens

Designer: Little Red Ant

Prepress technician: Margaret Salter

Print coordinator: Katherine Berti

Library and Archives Canada Cataloguing in Publication

Title: All kinds of bodies / written by Judith Heneghan ; illustrated by
  Ayesha Rubio and Jenny Palmer.
Names: Heneghan, Judith, 1965- author. | Rubio, Ayesha L.,
  illustrator. | Palmer, Jenny (Illustrator), illustrator.
Description: Series statement: All kinds of people |
  Previously published: London: Franklin Watts, 2019. |
  Includes index.
Identifiers: Canadiana (print) 20190200510 |
  Canadiana (ebook) 20190200529 |
  ISBN 9780778768012 (hardcover) |
  ISBN 9780778768050 (softcover) |
  ISBN 9781427124227 (HTML)
Subjects: LCSH: Human body—Juvenile literature.
Classification: LCC QP37 .H46 2020 | DDC j612—dc23

Library of Congress Cataloging-in-Publication Data

Names: Heneghan, Judith, 1965- author. | Lopez Rubio, Ayesha,
  illustrator. | Palmer, Jenny, illustrator.
Title: All kinds of bodies / written by Judith Heneghan ;
  illustrated by Ayesha Rubio and Jenny Palmer.
Description: New York, NY : Crabtree Publishing Company, 2020. |
  Series: All kinds of people | Includes index.
Identifiers: LCCN 2019043880 (print) | LCCN 2019043881 (ebook)
  ISBN 9780778768012 (hardcover) |
  ISBN 9780778768050 (paperback) |
  ISBN 9781427124227 (ebook)
Subjects: LCSH: Body image in children--Juvenile literature. |
  Human body--Social aspects--Juvenile literature. | Individual
  differences--Juvenile literature.
Classification: LCC BF723.B6 H46 2020 (print) |
  LCC BF723.B6 (ebook) | DDC 306.4/613--dc23
LC record available at https://lccn.loc.gov/2019043880
LC ebook record available at https://lccn.loc.gov/2019043881

Crabtree Publishing Company
www.crabtreebooks.com   1-800-387-7650
Published by Crabtree Publishing Company in 2020

Published in Canada
Crabtree Publishing
616 Welland Avenue
St. Catharines, ON
L2M 5V6

Published in the United States
Crabtree Publishing
PMB 59051
350 Fifth Ave, 59th Floor
New York, NY 10118

Printed in the U.S.A./012020/CG20191115

First published in Great Britain in 2019 by The Watts Publishing Group
Copyright © The Watts Publishing Group 2019

Contents

Bodies come in all kinds of shapes, colors, and sizes!

Bodies can be curved, straight, round, smooth, lumpy, muscly, thin, big, or little.

They also change as we get older.

Every shade or skin type needs protecting from the Sun.

Many of us grow hair on our heads and bodies.

Some might have
a little or a lot.

We can cover it, cut
it, color it—or not.

11

People from the same family may share similar **features**.

We are twins.

But not always!

Members of families can be different shapes and sizes, too.

Our bodies help us communicate and show others how we are feeling. Some people speak with their mouths.

Others speak with their hands.

Our bodies let us know what
we need, in all kinds of ways.

When I'm cold, my teeth chatter and my skin feels shivery.

When I'm tired, I yawn and fall asleep.

Most of us feel ill at some point in our lives.

Our bodies get sick or sore.

So we visit the doctor.

Some kinds of bodies
need a little extra help.

I have asthma, so sometimes I get out of breath and feel extra tired. My inhaler helps me recover.

Different bodies are good at different things.

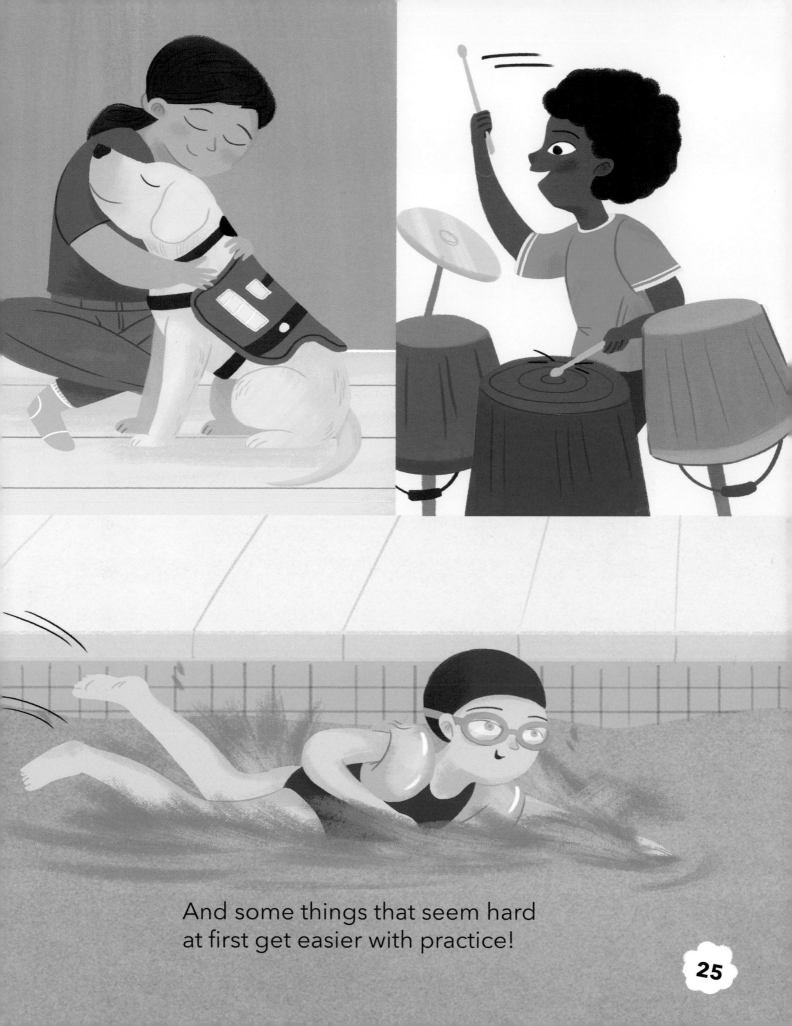

And some things that seem hard
at first get easier with practice!

Our differences make the world more interesting.

If our bodies were all the same, how would we recognize each other?

No one else has a body quite like mine or yours.

Every body is **unique**.

Every body
is amazing.

29

Notes for teachers, parents, and caregivers

This book is designed to help children feel good about their own bodies and value the wonderful diversity of people they encounter in the world around them. Children take their first cues about themselves and their peers from their parents or primary caregivers. If you are reading this book with a child in your care, encourage them to point out what they see in the pictures. Give them permission to be curious, to observe similarities and differences, and answer their questions with the following ideas in mind.

Be inclusive

Parents, teachers, and caregivers can help children appreciate all kinds of bodies by making sure the books they read and the programs they watch are as inclusive as possible. Normalize difference. Seek out positive role models for all children and celebrate each person's unique talents, regardless of gender, ethnicity, size, age, or disability. Show that the way we look does not define who we are. Point to the achievements of diverse sports stars, scientists, artists, or innovators who have challenged other people's preconceptions and prejudices.

Be positive

Children are helped to develop a positive body image when parents, teachers, and caregivers talk about their own bodies in positive ways. We can also encourage children to show us what they can do, and praise them when they try something new.

Challenge stereotypes

Stereotypes are lazy and misleading assumptions, such as "pink is for girls" or "boys prefer sports." Ask children whether they have come across any stereotypes they think are unfair. This is a good starting point for talking about the harm that stereotypes can do. Encourage open discussion about different kinds of bodies to help children develop empathy and challenge stereotypical assumptions about disability, gender, body shape, or ethnicity, for example.

Promote a healthy lifestyle

A healthy lifestyle isn't about looking different on the outside—it's about feeling good on the inside. A combination of a healthy, balanced diet and regular exercise helps children feel well and full of energy. It also helps them get a good night's sleep. Encourage positive actions, such as eating more fruits and vegetables, or taking up a fun new sport or hobby.

Your body belongs to you

Children need to learn that their body belongs to them and nobody else. This promotes self-esteem, and also gives them confidence to say no to unwelcome or inappropriate touching. Teachers can help by establishing clear boundaries for everyone in the classroom—no touching in any area covered by underwear, for example. All responsible adults need to be sensitive to signs of abuse that children may disclose in a classroom setting.

Activity—what do you see?

Ask a group of children to describe their own skin color and hair. Help them identify interesting words to describe color, shade, and texture. When each child has thought about themselves in this way, ask them to describe their neighbor with equal care. Follow this by suggesting they paint portraits of each other. This activity helps children learn about and appreciate the ways we are all different, and the same.

Useful words

asthma   An illness that makes your chest feel tight. People with asthma feel out of breath more easily.

birthmark   A patch of skin that is different in color or texture to the rest of your skin—something you have had since you were born

diabetes   An illness caused by too much sugar in your blood

features   The different parts of your face such as eyes, freckles, or wrinkles

inhaler   A device for giving medicine that helps people with asthma breathe more easily

sweat   The moisture on our skin when we feel hot

unique   Special, the only one of something

Index

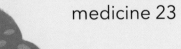